3 MINUTE
ITALIAN

LESSONS 4 – 6

KIERAN BALL

Mother Dearest...

I'd like to dedicate this book to my mum, who has given me so much in life, as well as life itself.

Thank you for your unequalled support, and thank you for being the one person in the world who has always held unwavering belief in everything I do.

You're the hardest working person I know and you have pushed me to be the greatest version of myself that I can be.

Ciao e benvenuto (hello and welcome) to "3 Minute Italian". I'm Kieran and I'm a language tutor based in the UK and I wrote this book to help you to learn to speak Italian.

The lessons in this book lead on from the last book "3 Minute Italian: Lessons 1-3". The methodology will get you speaking quickly, without the struggle normally associated with language learning.

I'll not bore you with my life story or intricate details of the history of the methodology; I know you probably just want to start learning Italian now, so I'll let you get on with it.

Actually, I've changed my mind, I will bore you a little before we start. It's my book! I'll keep it as brief as I can though.

I've been tutoring people for over ten years on a one-to-one basis in a range of subjects. I love languages, I love learning and I love teaching. I also love chocolate, but this isn't really the place to discuss my chocoholism. I'm very lucky that I get to teach people every day. However, I can't fit everybody who asks me into my schedule so, regrettably, I end up turning a lot of people away. I wish I could teach the whole world but I'm yet to figure out a way of duplicating myself!

The next best thing is to teach through the medium of a book. So, that's what I've decided to do. If you're reading this book, then I will soon be teaching you the glorious splendour that is the Italian language.

Anyway, I'll stop blathering on in a minute and we'll get started with learning. But, firstly, let me just say this...

Hullabaloo!

No, I'm joking, of course, let me say this instead...

We are all human beings, which means we all possess the attributes that make us human beings. There's a wonderful quote by a man called Terence:

"I am human, and nothing that is human is alien to me"

What it means is that if one person is capable of something, then we are all capable of it, because we're all humans too. There's nothing in the world that I cannot understand if somebody before me has succeeded in understanding it. Therefore, it's only logical that since there are more than 85 million people in the world who have managed to learn to speak Italian, then you can learn it too!

Anyway, philosophising over. Let's begin.

Contents

.

LESSON 4

Let's start this lesson with a quick recap of the words and phrases we learnt in the last lesson. How do you say the following in Italian?

always
that
that is...
perfect
thank you
yes
but

If there are any words you can't remember, go back to the last lesson and have a quick review of them before you start this lesson. It's really important that you remember the words you've learnt so far before you move on to learn any more.

Here's your first phrase in Italian for this lesson:

per lui

It means "for him"
You pronounce it "pair loo-wee"

How would you say these five sentences in Italian?

It's for him.

It's good for him.

It isn't for him.

It isn't very good for him.

It isn't for him; it's for me.

It's for him.
È per lui.

It's good for him.
È buono per lui.

It isn't for him.
Non è per lui.

It isn't very good for him.
Non è molto buono per lui.

It isn't for him; it's for me.
Non è per lui ; è per me.

This phrase goes nicely with "per lui" and "per me":

per lei

It means "for her"
You pronounce it "pair lay"

WORD LIST SO FAR

per lui – *for him*
per lei – *for her*

How would you say these three things in Italian?

It's for her.

Yes, it's very good for her.

It isn't for him; it's for her.

It's for her.
È per lei.

Yes, it's very good for her.
Si, è molto buono per lei.

It isn't for him; it's for her.
Non è per lui ; è per lei.

Here's your next word in Italian:

no

It means "no"
You pronounce it "noh"

WORD LIST SO FAR

per lui – *for him*
per lei – *for her*
no – *no*

How would you say these four sentences in Italian?

No, thank you.

No, it isn't for me; it's for her.

No, it isn't very good.

No, it isn't here.

No, thank you.
No, grazie.

No, it isn't for me; it's for her.
No, non è per me ; è per lei.

No, it isn't very good.
No, non è molto buono.

No, it isn't here.
No, non è qui.

Here's a new word for you. It's the opposite of
"buono":

cattivo

It means "bad"
You pronounce it "cat-ee-voh"

WORD LIST SO FAR

per lui – *for him*
per lei – *for her*
no – *no*
cattivo – *bad*

How would you say these four sentences in Italian?

It is always very bad here.

It isn't bad but it isn't perfect.

I think it's always bad here.

It's delicious but it's very bad for me.

It is always very bad here.
È sempre molto cattivo qui.

It isn't bad but it isn't perfect.
Non è cattivo ma non è perfetto.

I think it's always bad here.
Per me, è sempre cattivo qui.

It's delicious but it's very bad for
me.
È squisito ma è molto cattivo per
me.

Here's a word you'll probably recognise:

il ristorante

It means "the restaurant"
You pronounce it "eel ris-toh-ran-tay"

We've already had the phrase "non è" and learnt that it means "it isn't". Well, it has another meaning:

non è

It can also mean just "isn't"
You pronounce it "non ay"

So, how would you say the five sentences below in Italian?

The restaurant isn't here.

The restaurant isn't bad but it isn't fantastic.

Marco isn't here.

Maria isn't here.

The restaurant isn't perfect but it's very good.

The restaurant isn't here.
Il ristorante non è qui.

The restaurant isn't bad but it isn't fantastic.
Il ristorante non è cattivo ma non è fantastico.

Marco isn't here.
Marco non è qui.

Maria isn't here.
Maria non è qui.

The restaurant isn't perfect but it's very good.
Il ristorante non è perfetto ma è molto buono.

Similarly, we learnt that the word "è" means "it is":

è

Well, it can also mean just "is"
You pronounce it "ay"

WORD LIST SO FAR

per lui – *for him*
per lei – *for her*
no – *no*
cattivo – *bad*
il ristorante – *the restaurant*
non è – *isn't*
è – *is*

The restaurant is good.

The restaurant is here.

Maria is here.

Marco is here.

The restaurant is absolutely perfect.

The restaurant here is always very good.

The restaurant is good.
Il ristorante è buono.

The restaurant is here.
Il ristorante è qui.

Maria is here.
Maria è qui.

Marco is here.
Marco è qui.

The restaurant is absolutely perfect.
Il ristorante è assolutamente perfetto.

The restaurant here is always very good.
Il ristorante qui è sempre molto buono.

Here's your last word for this lesson:

tutto

It means "everything"
You pronounce it "too-toh"

WORD LIST SO FAR

per lui – *for him*
per lei – *for her*
no – *no*
cattivo – *bad*
il ristorante – *the restaurant*
non è – *isn't*
è – *is*
tutto – *everything*

How would you say these in Italian?

Everything is very good.

Everything is here.

Everything is delicious.

Everything is for me.

I think everything is perfect.

Everything is very bad for me but it's absolutely delicious.

Everything is very good.
Tutto è molto buono.

Everything is here.
Tutto è qui.

Everything is delicious.
Tutto è squisito.

Everything is for me.
Tutto è per me.

I think everything is perfect.
Per me, tutto è perfetto.

Everything is very bad for me but it's absolutely delicious.
Tutto è molto cattivo per me ma è assolutamente squisito.

It's time to practise what we've learnt in this lesson.
How do you say these sentences in Italian?

1. That is for him
2. The restaurant is absolutely extraordinary
3. That's the restaurant
4. Everything here is delicious
5. It isn't bad here
6. The restaurant is very good
7. I think the restaurant is fantastic
8. The restaurant is here
9. That is for her
10. Everything here is very good for me

1. Quello è per lui
2. Il ristorante è assolutamente straordinario
3. Quello è il ristorante
4. Tutto qui è squisito
5. Non è cattivo qui
6. Il ristorante è molto buono
7. Per me, il ristorante è fantastico
8. Il ristorante è qui
9. Quello è per lei
10. Tutto qui è molto buono per me

Now, let's have a go at doing some reverse translations.

1. Tutto è qui
2. Il ristorante qui è fantastico
3. Non è cattivo qui
4. Tutto è perfetto
5. Quello non è cattivo ma non è perfetto
6. Quello è per lui
7. Non è per lui ; è per me
8. Non è per lei ; è per lui
9. Non è molto buono per lui
10. Tutto è fantastico, grazie

1. Everything is here
2. The restaurant here is fantastic
3. It isn't bad here
4. Everything is perfect
5. That isn't bad but it isn't perfect
6. That is for him
7. It isn't for him; it's for me
8. It isn't for her; it's for him
9. It isn't very good for him
10. Everything is fantastic, thank you

What we're going to do now are some recap translations, which will incorporate words we learnt in the previous lesson.

1. It's very good, thank you
2. That isn't very good
3. It's for me, thank you
4. It's very beautiful here
5. That is very good
6. It's extraordinary
7. It's extraordinary here
8. It's absolutely delicious
9. I think it's good here
10. It's always fantastic here

1. È molto buono, grazie
2. Quello non è molto buono
3. È per me, grazie
4. È molto bello qui
5. Quello è molto buono
6. È straordinario
7. È straordinario qui
8. È assolutamente squisito
9. Per me, è buono qui
10. È sempre fantastico qui

Let's now do some Italian to English recap translations.

1. Si, è molto buono
2. È molto bello
3. Si, è assolutamente squisito
4. Per me, è fantastico
5. È sempre molto buono
6. Non è molto squisito
7. È sempre fantastico qui
8. Si, per me, è fantastico qui
9. È sempre molto bello qui
10. È per me

1. Yes, it's very good
2. It's very beautiful
3. Yes, it's absolutely delicious
4. I think it's fantastic
5. It's always very good
6. It isn't very delicious
7. It's always fantastic here
8. Yes, I think it's fantastic here
9. It's always very beautiful here
10. It's for me

Let's recap all the words we've learnt so far. How did you say these words in Italian?

1. the restaurant
2. beautiful
3. is
4. always
5. extraordinary
6. that is...
7. for her
8. it is
9. everything
10. delicious
11. absolutely
12. perfect
13. but
14. it isn't
15. no
16. yes
17. isn't
18. for him
19. I think
20. good
21. very
22. for me
23. that
24. fantastic
25. here
26. thank you

2. il ristorante
3. bello
4. è
5. sempre
6. straordinario
7. quello è
8. per lei
9. è
10. tutto
11. squisito
12. absolutamente
13. perfetto
14. ma

15. non è
16. no
17. si
18. non è
19. per lui
20. per me
21. buono
22. molto
23. per me
24. quello
25. fantastico
26. qui
27. grazie

LESSON 5

Let's start this lesson with a quick recap of the words and phrases we learnt in the last lesson. How do you say the following in Italian?

for him
isn't
no
for her
everything
bad
the restaurant
is

If there are any words you can't remember, go back to the last lesson and have a quick review of them before you start this lesson. It's really important that you remember the words you've learnt so far before you move on to learn any more.

Here's a nice word with which to start this lesson:

il pollo

It means "the chicken"
You pronounce it "eel poll-oh"

How would you say these five sentences in Italian?

The chicken is for me.

I think the chicken here is delicious.

The chicken is for him.

The chicken is very good.

The chicken here is always absolutely fantastic.

The chicken is for me.
Il pollo è per me.

I think the chicken here is delicious.
Per me, il pollo qui è squisito.

The chicken is for him.
Il pollo è per lui.

The chicken is very good.
Il pollo è molto buono.

The chicken here is always absolutely fantastic.
Il pollo qui è sempre assolutamente fantastico.

So, "il pollo" means "the chicken" and here's another word you'll probably recognise:

la pizza

It means "the pizza"
You pronounce it "la peet-sah"

WORD LIST SO FAR

il pollo – *the chicken*
la pizza – *the pizza*

How would you say the following three sentences in Italian?

The pizza is for her.

The pizza is here.

The pizza isn't for me.

The pizza is for her.
La pizza è per lei.

The pizza is here.
La pizza è qui.

The pizza isn't for me.
La pizza non è per me.

You may have noticed that I've used two different words for "the" in this lesson. I said "<u>il</u> pollo" means "<u>the</u> chicken" and then I said "<u>la</u> pizza" means "<u>the</u> pizza". Well, there's an interesting thing about the word "the" in Italian. Read on...

the

In Italian, there are two words for "the". One is used in front of masculine nouns, and the other is used in front of feminine nouns.

If you use a masculine noun, you have to use 'il, if you use a feminine noun, you have to use 'la'.

il
the (masculine)
la
the (feminine)

How do you know when a noun is masculine or feminine?

Sometimes, you can guess. For example, you can probably guess that "boy" is masculine and "girl" is feminine:

il ragazzo
the boy
la ragazza
the girl

However, it's not always so simple; nouns like "table" or "car" don't have real genders.

There is a rule, however, that you can use to work out whether something is masculine or feminine. This rule works about 90% of the time. If a noun ends in the letter A, it's probably feminine.

Look at the five nouns below. The two feminine nouns end in the letter A and the three masculine nouns don't. Usually, masculine nouns end in the letter O, but not always:

il ragazzo
the boy

il ristorante
the restaurant

il pollo
the chicken

la ragazz<u>a</u>
the girl

la pizz<u>a</u>
the pizza

So, just remember the general rule: if a noun ends in the letter A, it's probably feminine.

What's a noun?

I remember when I started to learn languages, the teacher would throw around these fancy words: noun, adjective, verb and adverb, and I had no idea what she meant.

Here's the simplest definition of a noun that I could find:

"If you can put 'the' in front of a word, then it's most probably a noun"

The restaurant
The chicken
The pizza

So, that means that words you can put "il" or "la" in front of in Italian are nouns.

How would you say this in Italian?

The chicken is good.

The chicken is good.
Il pollo è buono.

buono

The word "good" is used to describe things. This is because it's an adjective and adjectives describe things.

If you use "good" to describe something masculine in Italian, then you can use "buono", as we have already seen.

However, if you want to say that something feminine is good, the word "buono" changes slightly, and becomes "buona".

So, bearing in mind that "pizza" is a feminine noun, how would you say, "the pizza is good"?

La pizza è <u>buona</u>

So, you use "buono" when talking about masculine things, and you use "buona" when talking about feminine things.

WORD LIST SO FAR

il pollo – *the chicken*
la pizza – *the pizza*
il / la – *the (masculine / feminine)*
buono / buona – *good (masculine / feminine)*

How would you say these four sentences in Italian?

The chicken is good.

The pizza is good.

Marco is good.

Maria is good.

The chicken is good.
Il pollo è buono.

The pizza is good.
La pizza è buona.

Marco is good.
Marco è buono.

Maria is good.
Maria è buona.

So, the feminine version of "buono" is "buona":

buona

It means "good" when you're describing feminine
things
You pronounce it "bwo-na"

buono vs. buona

So, you use "buono" when you're describing masculine nouns, and "buona" when you're describing feminine nouns.

"Buono" isn't the only adjective that can change when describing a feminine noun. Some of the other adjectives we've learn can change too. Usually, what happens is, if an adjective ends in the letter O, you change the O to an A to make it feminine.

I remember this by thinking of the two names Mario and Maria. Mario is a man's name and it ends in an O, whereas Maria is a woman's name and it ends in an A.

Read on...

What's an adjective?

An adjective is a word that is used to describe something. However, a simpler explanation is this:

If you can put "it is" in front of a word, then it's most probably an adjective.

It is good
It is fantastic
It is delicious
It is perfect
It is bad

The words above are adjectives.

The Italian word for "delicious" is "squisito". When you use it to describe a feminine noun, it changes slightly to become "squisita":

squisita

It means "delicious" when you're describing feminine things
You pronounce it "skwizz-ee-ta"

How would you say these two things in Italian?

The chicken is delicious.

The pizza is delicious.

The chicken is delicious.
Il pollo è squisito.

The pizza is delicious.
La pizza è squisita.

The Italian word for "perfect" is "perfetto". When you use it to describe a feminine noun, it changes slightly to become "perfetta":

perfetta

It means "perfect" when you're describing feminine things
You pronounce it "pair-fett-ah"

WORD LIST SO FAR

il pollo – *the chicken*
la pizza – *the pizza*
il / la – *the (masculine / feminine)*
buono / buona – *good (masculine / feminine)*
squisito / squisita – *delicious (masculine / feminine)*
perfetto / perfetta – *perfect (masculine / feminine)*

How would you say the two sentences below in Italian?

The chicken is perfect.

The pizza is perfect.

The chicken is delicious.
Il pollo è squisito.

The pizza is delicious.
La pizza è squisita.

The Italian word for "bad" is "cattivo". When you use it to describe a feminine noun, it changes slightly to become "cattiva":

cattiva

It means "bad" when you're describing feminine things
You pronounce it "catt-ee-vah"

WORD LIST SO FAR

il pollo – *the chicken*
la pizza – *the pizza*
il / la – *the (masculine / feminine)*
buono / buona – *good (masculine / feminine)*
squisito / squisita – *delicious (masculine / feminine)*
perfetto / perfetta – *perfect (masculine / feminine)*
cattivo / cattiva – *bad (masculine / feminine)*

How would you say these four sentences in Italian?

The chicken is bad.

The pizza is bad.

Marco is bad.

Maria is bad.

The chicken is bad.
Il pollo è cattivo.

The pizza is bad.
La pizza è cattiva.

Marco is bad.
Marco è cattivo.

Maria is bad.
Maria è cattiva.

masculine & feminine

So far, we've seen how four adjectives change if they're describing feminine nouns. You just change the O on the end to an A:

buono – buona
squisito – squisita
perfetto – perfetta
cattivo – cattiva

Here are another couple of adjectives:

fantastico – fantastica
bello – bella

WORD LIST SO FAR

il pollo – *the chicken*
la pizza – *the pizza*
il / la – *the (masculine / feminine)*
buono / buona – *good (masculine / feminine)*
squisito / squisita – *delicious (masculine / feminine)*
perfetto / perfetta – *perfect (masculine / feminine)*
cattivo / cattiva – *bad (masculine / feminine)*
fantastico / fantastica – *fantastic (masculine / feminine)*
bello / bella – *beautiful (masculine / feminine)*

How would you say the sentences below in Italian?

The chicken is fantastic.

The pizza is fantastic.

Marco is beautiful.

Maria is beautiful.

The chicken is fantastic.
Il pollo è fantastico.

The pizza is fantastic.
La pizza è fantastica.

Marco is beautiful.
Marco è bello.

Maria is beautiful.
Maria è bella.

Here's a word that looks very similar to the English:

terribile

It means "terrible"
You pronounce it "the-ree-billay"

WORD LIST SO FAR

il pollo – *the chicken*
la pizza – *the pizza*
il / la – *the (masculine / feminine)*
buono / buona – *good (masculine / feminine)*
squisito / squisita – *delicious (masculine / feminine)*
perfetto / perfetta – *perfect (masculine / feminine)*
cattivo / cattiva – *bad (masculine / feminine)*
fantastico / fantastica – *fantastic (masculine / feminine)*
bello / bella – *beautiful (masculine / feminine)*
terribile – *terrible*

So, how would you say this in Italian?

The restaurant is terrible.

The restaurant is terrible.
Il ristorante è terribile.

terribile

The word "terribile" in Italian ends in the letter E and not the letter O, like most adjectives. When this happens, the feminine version of the adjective tends to be the same as the masculine. It doesn't change at all.

This is true with "terribile"; whether you're describing masculine or feminine things as terrible, you always just use "terribile".

WORD LIST SO FAR

il pollo – *the chicken*
la pizza – *the pizza*
il / la – *the (masculine / feminine)*
buono / buona – *good (masculine / feminine)*
squisito / squisita – *delicious (masculine / feminine)*
perfetto / perfetta – *perfect (masculine / feminine)*
cattivo / cattiva – *bad (masculine / feminine)*
fantastico / fantastica – *fantastic (masculine / feminine)*
bello / bella – *beautiful (masculine / feminine)*
terribile – *terrible*

How would you say these five sentences in Italian?

The pizza is terrible.

It's terrible here.

I think it's absolutely terrible.

It's always terrible here.

It isn't perfect but it isn't terrible.

The pizza is terrible.
La pizza è terribile.

It's terrible here.
È terribile qui.

I think it's absolutely terrible.
Per me, è assolutamente terribile.

It's always terrible here.
È sempre terribile qui.

It isn't perfect but it isn't terrible.
Non è perfetto ma non è terribile.

Food, glorious food

Now, if you go on holiday, I presume you'll want to order something other than chicken or pizza. So, I've created a list of food related vocabulary for you to read through. I've called it a "Vocabulary Expansion Section" and you'll find it at the end of this lesson.

I've tried to think of as many food or drink items as I possibly could. If you find anything missing, let me know and I'll add it in.

This Vocabulary Expansion Section will add bulk to your Italian language. You have been building the structure of the Italian language with the words and phrases I've given you so far and you can now decorate it and embellish it with the words from the Vocabulary Expansion Section.

Now, obviously, you shouldn't aim to try and learn every single word on the list as it wouldn't be very useful and it would take a long time. Instead, start to build your own personal vocabulary by learning a few words you think you'll learn regularly. For example, if you really love cheese, you can find and learn the word "il formaggio". Add a few words every week or so and pretty soon you'll have a nice collection in your brain.

It's time to practise what we've learnt in this lesson.

1. Everything is terrible
2. The chicken is absolutely delicious
3. The chicken is absolutely terrible
4. The chicken is very good
5. The pizza is very good
6. The pizza is for her
7. The pizza is perfect
8. The chicken is delicious
9. The pizza is for me
10. The pizza is delicious

1. Tutto è terribile
2. Il pollo è assolutamente squisito
3. Il pollo è assolutamente terribile
4. Il pollo è molto buono
5. La pizza è molto buona
6. La pizza è per lei
7. La pizza è perfetta
8. Il pollo è squisito
9. La pizza è per me
10. La pizza è squisita

Now, let's have a go at doing some reverse translations.

1. La pizza è molto buona
2. Tutto è terribile
3. Il pollo è fantastico
4. Il pollo è molto buono
5. Il pollo è perfetto
6. Il pollo è assolutamente terribile
7. La pizza è squisita
8. Il pollo è molto buono ma la pizza è straordinaria
9. La pizza è per me
10. Tutto è sempre terribile qui

1. The pizza is very good
2. Everything is terrible
3. The chicken is fantastic
4. The chicken is very good
5. The chicken is perfect
6. The chicken is absolutely terrible
7. The pizza is delicious
8. The chicken is very good but the pizza is extraordinary
9. The pizza is for me
10. Everything is always terrible here

What we're going to do now are some recap translations, which will incorporate words we learnt in the previous lessons.

1. I think it's absolutely fantastic
2. It's absolutely beautiful
3. It's fantastic
4. It isn't here
5. That isn't very good
6. It's for me
7. It isn't for her
8. It's always very beautiful here
9. That for me, thank you
10. I think it's good

1. Per me, è assolutamente fantastico
2. È assolutamente bello
3. È fantastico
4. Non è qui
5. Quello non è molto buono
6. È per me
7. Non è per lei
8. È sempre molto bello qui
9. Quello per me, grazie
10. Per me, è buono

Let's now do some Italian to English recap translations.

1. Quello non è molto buono
2. Non è sempre buono qui
3. Non è buono qui
4. È straordinario
5. Si, è per me
6. Tutto è qui
7. Il ristorante non è cattivo
8. Quello non è cattivo ma non è perfetto
9. Non è molto buono per lei
10. Quello è per lei

1. That isn't very good
2. It isn't always good here
3. It isn't good here
4. It's extraordinary
5. Yes, it's for me
6. Everything is here
7. The restaurant isn't bad
8. That isn't bad but it isn't perfect
9. It isn't very good for her
10. That is for her

Let's recap all the words we've learnt so far. How did you say these words in Italian?

1. isn't
2. is
3. for him
4. good
5. it isn't
6. yes
7. extraordinary
8. very
9. the chicken
10. fantastic
11. the restaurant
12. but
13. for me
14. everything
15. I think
16. thank you
17. always
18. perfect
19. terrible
20. for her
21. no
22. that is...
23. it is
24. beautiful
25. absolutely
26. that
27. the pizza
28. here
29. delicious

2. non è
3. è
4. per lui
5. buono
6. non è
7. si
8. straordinario
9. molto
10. il pollo
11. fantastico
12. il ristorante
13. ma
14. per me
15. tutto
16. per me

17. grazie
18. sempre
19. perfetto
20. terribile
21. per lei
22. no
23. quello è...
24. è
25. bello
26. assolutamente
27. quello
28. la pizza
29. qui
30. squisito

LESSON 6

Let's start this lesson with a quick recap of the words and phrases we learnt in the last lesson. How do you say the following in Italian?

the chicken
the pizza
the (masculine / feminine)
good (masculine / feminine)
delicious (masculine / feminine)
perfect (masculine / feminine)
bad (masculine / feminine)
fantastic (masculine / feminine)
beautiful (masculine / feminine)
terrible

If there are any words you can't remember, go back to the last lesson and have a quick review of them before you start this lesson. It's really important that you remember the words you've learnt so far before you move on to learn any more.

Here's your first word for this lesson:

il mio

It means "my"
You pronounce it "eel meeoh"

How would you say these four sentences in Italian?

My chicken is delicious.

My restaurant is here.

My chicken is here.

My chicken is very good.

My chicken is delicious.
Il mio pollo è squisito.

My restaurant is here.
Il mio ristorante è qui.

My chicken is here.
Il mio pollo è qui.

My chicken is very good.
Il mio pollo è molto buono.

Here's your next Italian word:

l'albergo

It means "the hotel"
You pronounce it "lal-bear-goh

l'albergo

You might have noticed that there is a little L' in front of the word "albergo". This is called a contraction.

It's a short version of the word IL.

Whenever you put the words IL or LA in front of a word that starts with a vowel in Italian, it becomes shortened to L' like in the word l'albergo.

This is purely because "l'albergo" is easier to say than "il albergo".

How would you say the following three sentences in Italian?

The hotel is very good.

The hotel isn't bad.

My hotel is fantastic.

The hotel is very good.
L'albergo è molto buono.

The hotel isn't bad.
L'albergo non è cattivo.

My hotel is fantastic.
Il mio albergo è fantastico.

Here's a useful phrase in Italian:

ognuno

It means "everybody" or "everyone"
You pronounce it "on-yunoh"

gn

Whenever you see the letters GN together, imagine instead that it's an NY. That's how you pronounce it.

Imagine the word "lasagna", you pronounce it "lazanya" as if the GN were an NY.

So, "ognuno" is pronounced "onyunoh"

How would you say the three sentences below in Italian?

Everybody is here.

Everybody is fantastic.

Everybody is always fantastic here.

Everybody is here.
Ognuno è qui.

Everybody is fantastic.
Ognuno è fantastico.

Everybody is always fantastic here.
Ognuno è sempre fantastico qui.

Here's a nice word:

simpatico

It means "nice"
You pronounce it "sim-pah-tee-koh"

WORD LIST SO FAR

il mio – *my*
l'albergo – *the hotel*
ognuno – *everybody / everyone*
simpatico – *nice*

How would you say the sentences below in Italian?

It's nice here.

Everybody is nice.

Everybody here is nice.

Everybody here is always very nice.

It's nice here.
È simpatico qui.

Everybody is nice.
Ognuno è simpatico.

Everybody here is nice.
Ognuno qui è simpatico.

Everybody here is always very nice.
Ognuno qui è sempre molto
simpatico.

Italian MY

We learnt last lesson that the Italians have two words for "the": IL and LA.

Well, the Italians also have two words for "my": IL MIO for masculine words, and LA MIA for feminine words.

il mio
my (masculine)

la mia
my (feminine)

So, you use "il mio" in front of masculine nouns and "la mia" in front of feminine nouns. For example:

il mio pollo – my chicken
la mia pizza – my pizza

How would you say these six sentences in Italian?

My chicken is good.

My pizza is delicious.

My hotel is terrible.

My pizza is very bad.

My pizza is absolutely perfect.

My chicken is absolutely perfect.

My chicken is good.
Il mio pollo è buono.

My pizza is delicious.
La mia pizza è squisita.

My hotel is terrible.
Il mio albergo è terribile.

My pizza is very bad.
La mia pizza è molto cattiva.

My pizza is absolutely perfect.
La mia pizza è assolutamente
perfetta.

My chicken is absolutely perfect.
Il mio pollo è assolutamente
perfetto.

It's time to practise what we've learnt in this lesson.

1. My hotel is very good
2. The hotel is very good
3. That is my pizza
4. My hotel isn't very good
5. Everybody is here
6. The hotel is fantastic
7. Everybody is very nice
8. The hotel is terrible
9. The hotel is terrible but the restaurant is extraordinary
10. My pizza is delicious

1. Il mio albergo è molto buono
2. L'albergo è molto buono
3. Quello è la mia pizza
4. Il mio albergo non è molto buono
5. Ognuno è qui
6. L'albergo è fantastico
7. Ognuno è molto simpatico
8. L'albergo è terribile
9. L'albergo è terribile ma il ristorante è straordinario
10. La mia pizza è squisita

Now, let's have a go at doing some reverse translations.

1. Il mio albergo è molto buono
2. La mia pizza è perfetta
3. Il mio pollo è terribile
4. Quello non è il mio pollo
5. Per me, ognuno è molto simpatico
6. Il mio pollo è qui
7. L'albergo è molto buono
8. L'albergo è fantastico
9. Ognuno è qui
10. Ognuno è sempre simpatico qui

1. My hotel is very good
2. My pizza is perfect
3. My chicken is terrible
4. That isn't my chicken
5. I think everybody is very nice
6. My chicken is here
7. The hotel is very good
8. The hotel is fantastic
9. Everybody is here
10. Everybody is always nice here

What we're going to do now are some recap translations, which will incorporate words we learnt in the previous lessons.

1. It isn't very good for me
2. The restaurant is very good
3. It's very good, thank you
4. It isn't good; it's fantastic
5. The chicken is fantastic
6. It isn't delicious
7. That's the chicken
8. That isn't very good
9. Not for me
10. It's always absolutely perfect

1. Non è molto buono per me
2. Il ristorante è molto buono
3. È molto buono, grazie
4. Non è buono ; è fantastico
5. Il pollo è fantastico
6. Non è squisito
7. Quello è il pollo
8. Quello non è molto buono
9. Non per me
10. È sempre assolutamente perfetto

Let's now do some Italian to English recap translations.

1. Non è per lei ; è per lui
2. Il ristorante è assolutamente straordinario
3. Tutto è perfetto
4. Per me, la pizza è assolutamente perfetta
5. Non è per lei ; è per me
6. Il ristorante qui è fantastico
7. È assolutamente squisito
8. Non è per me
9. È sempre qui
10. È sempre fantastico qui

1. It isn't for her; it's for him
2. The restaurant is absolutely extraordinary
3. Everything is perfect
4. I think the pizza is absolutely perfect
5. It isn't for her; it's for me
6. The restaurant here is fantastic
7. It's absolutely delicious
8. It isn't for me
9. It's always here
10. It's always fantastic here

Let's recap all the words we've learnt so far. How did you say these words in Italian?

1. very
2. is
3. but
4. beautiful
5. delicious
6. the hotel
7. everything
8. my
9. it isn't
10. absolutely
11. that is...
12. yes
13. the chicken
14. good
15. for her
16. nice
17. it is
18. extraordinary
19. perfect
20. no
21. here
22. the pizza
23. for me
24. thank you
25. everybody
26. fantastic
27. I think
28. that
29. terrible
30. always
31. for him
32. the restaurant
33. isn't

1. molto
2. è
3. ma
4. bello
5. squisito
6. l'albergo
7. tutto
8. il mio
9. non è
10. assolutamente
11. quello è...
12. sì
13. il pollo
14. buono
15. per lei
16. simpatico
17. è
18. straordinario
19. perfetto
20. non
21. qui
22. la pizza
23. per me
24. grazie
25. ognuno
26. fantastico
27. per me
28. quello
29. terribile
30. sempre
31. per lui
32. il ristorante
33. non è

Vocabulary Expansion Section

Al ristorante

at the restaurant

l'insalata

una cetriolo
una lattuga
un cipolla
un pomodoro
il sedano
un peperone
i spinaci
un ravanello
una barbabietola
il crescione
il condimento per l'insalata
un crostino

the salad

a cucumber
a lettuce
an onion
a tomato
celery
a pepper
the spinach
a radish
a beetroot
the cress
the salad dressing
a crouton

la carne

l'agnello
la bistecca
  ben cotto
  di cottura media
  poco cotto
  al sangue
la tacchino
il prosciutto

the meat

the lamb
the steak
  well done
  medium-rare
  rare
  blue
the turkey
the ham

la carne di maiale	the pork
il pollo	the chicken
il manzo	the beef
il salame/ la salsiccia	the sausage
l'anatra	the duck
il coniglio	the rabbit
il vitello	the veal
il cervo	the venison
la faraona	the guinea-fowl
la quaglia	the quail
un fegato	a liver
un rognone	a kidney

il pesce / *the fish*

il salmone	the salmon
il tonno	the tuna
la trota	the trout
il merluzzo	the cod
l'eglefino	the haddock
la platessa	the plaice
la sogliola	the sole
la rana pescatrice	the monkfish

le verdure / *the vegetables*

una carota	a carrot
un fungo	a mushroom
un cavolfiore	a cauliflower
un fagiolo	a bean
il mais dolce	the sweetcorn

i bisi	the peas
una patata	a potato
un cavolo	a cabbage
gli asparagi	the asparagus
i broccoli	the broccoli
un porro	a leek
una melanzana	an aubergine
un fagiolo di spagna	a runner bean
un fagiolino	a green bean
il pisello mangiatutto	the mangetout
una pastinaca	a parsnip
una zucca	a pumpkin
un zucchino	a marrow
una zucchina	a courgette
un cetriolino	a gherkin
un cavolo di bruxelles	a brussels sprout
un carciofo	an artichoke
una rapa	a turnip
un navone	a swede
una patata dolce	a sweet potato
un cece	a chickpea
una lenticchia	a lentil
un seme di soia	a soy bean

i frutti di mare

un gambaretto
un gambero
i scampi
un'ostrica
una cozza
un'astice
un ganchio
un calamaro
un polpo
una acciuga

the seafood

a prawn
a large prawn
the scampi
an oyster
a mussel
a lobster
a crab
a squid/ calamari
an octopus
an anchovy

le alter cose

il patè
il formaggio
un uovo sodo
un uovo alla coque
un uovo fritto
l'uovo strapazzate
una frittata
la minestra
i cereali
il porridge
il riso
la pasta
le taglietelle
le patate fritte
le patatine
un cocktail di gamberetti

the other things

the pâté
the cheese
a hard-boiled egg
a soft boiled egg
a fried egg
scrambled eggs
an omelette
the soup
the cereal
the porridge
the rice
the pasta
the noodles
the chips
the crisps
the prawn cocktail

un panino	a sandwich
un hamburger	a hamburger
un hot dog	a hot dog
un kebab	a kebab

i condimenti ecc... — *the condiments etc...*

il sale	the salt
il pepe	the pepper
l'aceto	the vinegar
la senape	the mustard
la salsa di menta	the mint sauce
il zucchero	the sugar
il dolcificante	the sweetener
il miele	the honey
l'aglio	the garlic
la marmellata	the marmalade
il ketchup	the tomato sauce
la salsa hp	the brown sauce
la salsa di soia	the soy sauce
la maionese	the mayonnaise
l'olio (d'oliva)	the (olive) oil
la maionese all'aglio	the garlic mayonnaise
il burro	the butter
il pane (bianco)	the (white) bread
(...integrale)	(brown...)
il pane tostato	the toast
il yogurt	the yoghurt

le dolce	*the desserts*
una torta	a cake
il gelato	an ice cream
alla fragola	*strawberry*
alla vaniglia	*vanilla*
al cioccolato	*chocolate*
alla menta	*mint*
alla menta con scaglie di cioccolato	
	mint choc chip
i dolciumi	the sweets
un crêpe	a pancake
il cioccolato	the chocolate
una torta	a pie
la panna	the cream
un biscotto	a biscuit
un cracker	a cracker
una tortina	a muffin
la crema pasticcera	the custard
un tiramisù	a tiramisu
una mousse	a mousse
il rabarbaro	the rhubarb
una macedonia	a fruit cocktail
un'insalata di frutta	a fruit salad

la frutta

the fruit

un'ananas	a pineapple
una banana	a banana
una fragola	a strawberry
un lampone	a raspberry
un'arancia	an orange
un pompelmo	a grapefruit
un'anguria	a watermelon
una pesca	a peach
una pera	a pear
una mela	an apple
un'uva	a grape
un mirtillo	a blueberry
una pesca nettarina	a nectarine
una prugna/ susina	a plum
un limone	a lemon
una limetta	a lime
una clementina	a clementine
un satsuma	a satsuma
un tangerino	a tangerine
un'albicocca	an apricot
una ciliegia	a cherry
una mora	a blackberry
una bacca di ginepro	a juniper berry
un'avocado	an avocado
un ribes nero	a blackcurrant
un dattero	a date
un pitaya	a dragonfruit
un frutto della passione	a passion fruit

un'uva spina	a gooseberry
una guaiava	a guava
un kiwi	a kiwi
un kumquat	a kumquat
un litchi	a lychee
un mango	a mango
un melone	a melon
un melone d'inverno	a honeydew melon
un melone di cantalupo	a cantaloupe
una melagrana	a pomegranate
una fisaglia	a physalis
un mirtillo rosso	a cranberry
un'arachide	a peanut
una noce	a walnut
un pistacchio	a pistachio

le bevande

un caffè	a coffee
latte	with milk
un tè	a tea
un'acqua	a water
gassata	*sparkling*
naturale	*still*
del rubinetto	*tap*
un succo (di frutta)	a (fruit) juice
un'acua tonica	a tonic water
una coca	a cola
il latte	the milk
una limonata	a lemonade
...dietetico	diet...
un vino	a wine
rosso	*red*
bianco	*white*
rosato	*rosé*
una birra	a beer
una birra bionda	a lager
un sidro	a cider
un sherry	a sherry
un brandy	a brandy
un whisky	a whisky
un gin	a gin
un liquore	a liqueur
un vermut	a vermouth
un rum	a rum
con ghiaccio	with ice

le postate	*the cutlery*
un coltello	a knife
un cucchiaio	a spoon
un cucchiaino	a teaspoon
un cucchiaio da minestra	a soup spoon
una forchetta	a fork
un piatto	a plate
una scodella	a bowl
una tazza	a cup
un bicchiere	a glass
un stuzzicadenti	a toothpick
un tovagliolo	a napkin
un secchiello del ghiaccio	an ice bucket
una caraffa d'acqua	a waterjug

Grazie

Before you go, I'd like to say "grazie" for buying this book. There are lots of Italian books available on Amazon and you chose to read mine, so I am eternally grateful for that.

I hope you have enjoyed this book and I hope you're glad you made the purchase. I also hope you've started to realise how easy learning a new language can be.

This book contained lessons four to six of my "3 Minute Italian" course. If you would like to learn more, you can get the next book in the series containing lessons seven to nine, and further books after that to continue building your Italian language skills.

For more information on where to get the next books, or if you'd like any more tips on language learning, you can visit my website www.3minute.club

Thank you again, grazie e a dopo!

17475123R00070

Printed in Great Britain
by Amazon